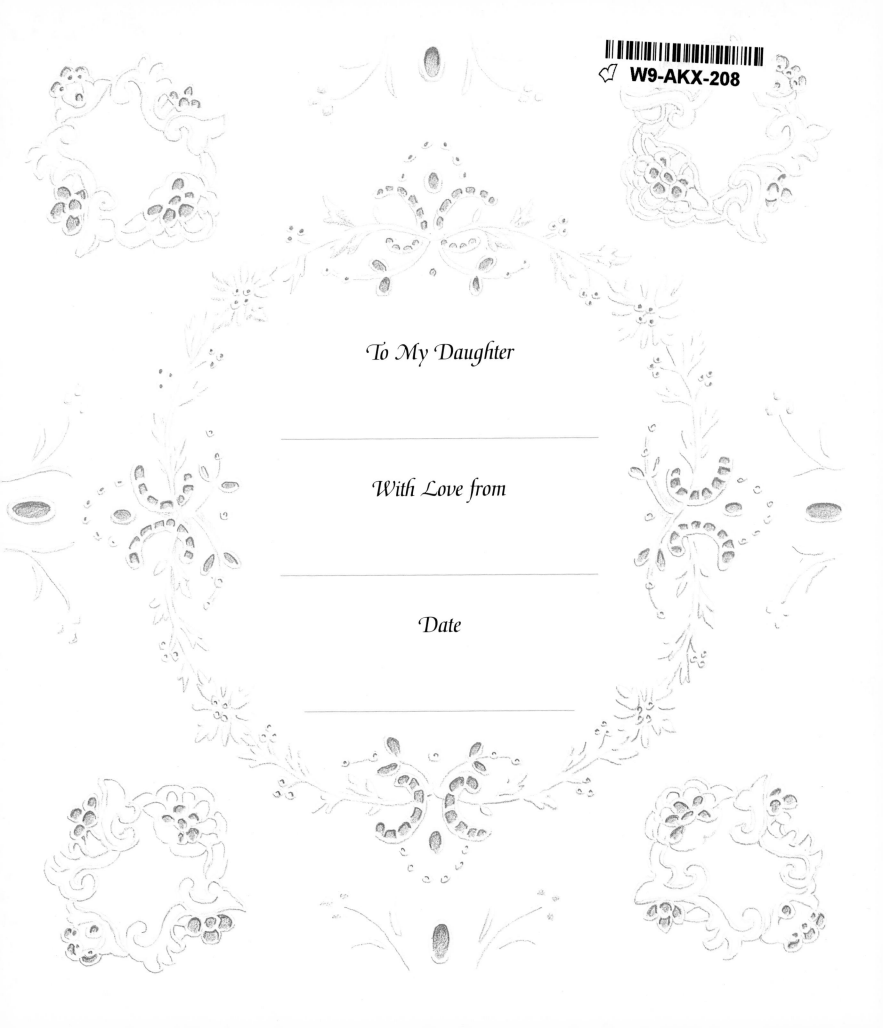

To My Daughter

_____

With Love from

_____

Date

_____

To My Daughter, With Love

A MOTHER'S MEMORY BOOK

Written and Illustrated by
DONNA GREEN

VERMILION

This edition published in 1993 by Vermilion, Inc.
P.O. Box 176, Cohasset, MA 02025

Would you like to own a limited-edition, signed and numbered reproduction of a painting by artist/illustrator Donna Green? For information write to:
Donna Green, c/o Vermilion, Box 176, Cohasset, MA 02025.

This Vermilion edition is distributed through gift stores by
Pictura, Inc., 4 Andrews Drive, West Paterson, NJ 07424

A Rob Fremont Book

Design by Carol Belanger Grafton
Editor: Pati Cockram
Composition: Trufont Typographers, Inc.
Composition: Garbo Typesetting

ISBN: 1-883746-01-9

Printed and bound in Spain by Bookprint, S.L.

20 19 18 17 16 15 14 13 12

To my mother,
who encouraged me to dream,
and to my daughter Monique,
my dream come true.

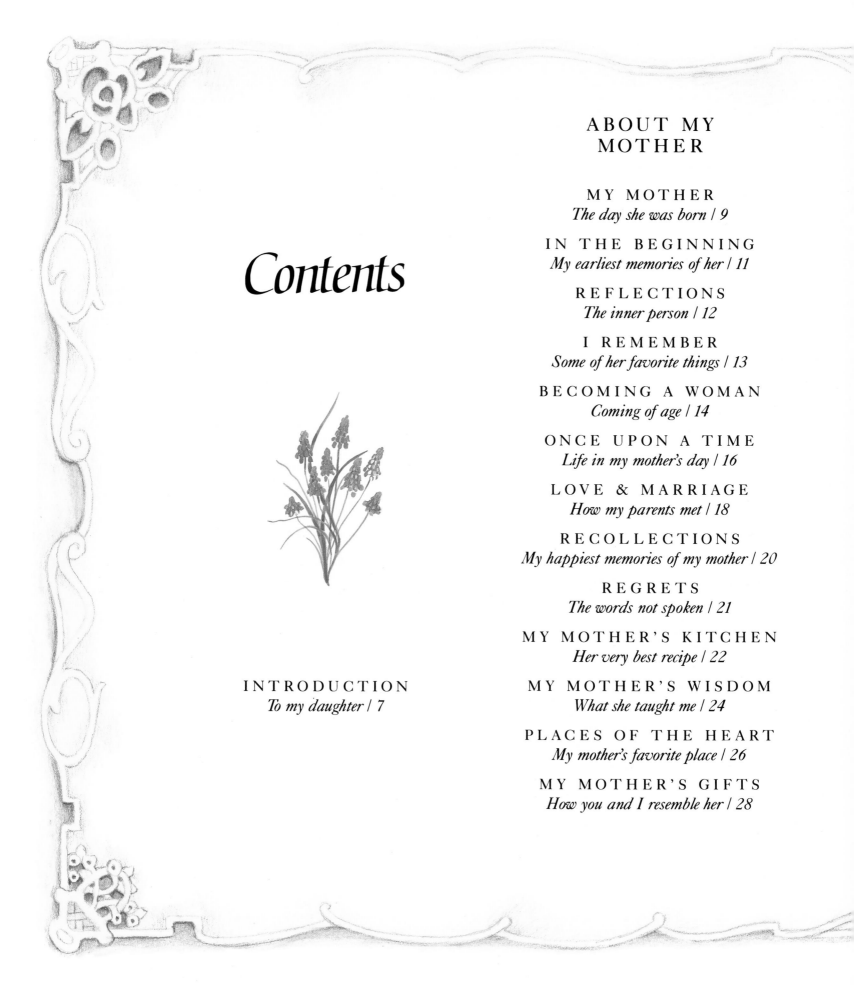

Contents

ABOUT MY
MOTHER

MY MOTHER
The day she was born | 9

IN THE BEGINNING
My earliest memories of her | 11

REFLECTIONS
The inner person | 12

I REMEMBER
Some of her favorite things | 13

BECOMING A WOMAN
Coming of age | 14

ONCE UPON A TIME
Life in my mother's day | 16

LOVE & MARRIAGE
How my parents met | 18

RECOLLECTIONS
My happiest memories of my mother | 20

REGRETS
The words not spoken | 21

MY MOTHER'S KITCHEN
Her very best recipe | 22

MY MOTHER'S WISDOM
What she taught me | 24

PLACES OF THE HEART
My mother's favorite place | 26

MY MOTHER'S GIFTS
How you and I resemble her | 28

INTRODUCTION
To my daughter | 7

ABOUT MYSELF

ABOUT MYSELF
The day I was born | 31

WHEN I WAS VERY YOUNG
My earliest recollections | 33

MY HOME TOWN
Our house and street | 35

SCHOOL DAYS
My warmest memories | 36

DAYDREAMS
How I visualized the future | 39

MY ROOM
Why it was special to me | 40

DEAR DIARY
Secrets | 41

BOYS
My first romance | 42

THE LITTLE THINGS
Some of my strongest memories | 44

MY PASSIONS
A few of my favorite things | 46

WONDERFUL WORDS
Words that have meant so much | 47

LOVE CONQUERS ALL
Romantic recollections | 48

MY WEDDING
Love and marriage | 49

THEN THERE WAS YOU
The day I learned I was pregnant | 51

ABOUT MY DAUGHTER

MY DAUGHTER
The day you were born | 53

WHEN YOU WERE LITTLE
Special memories | 54

FIRST WINGS
Your first day of school | 56

SPECIAL MEMORIES
Remembering those wonderful years | 58

MOM'S APPLE PIE
A mother's gift: my best recipe | 59

ALL GROWN UP
It happened so quickly | 60

WHEN WE BECAME FRIENDS
Our special relationship | 62

MR. RIGHT
The man of your dreams | 64

YOUR WEDDING
If ever two were one | 65

THE BEST OF TIMES
Do you remember? | 66

PRIVATE THOUGHTS
My dreams for you | 68

YOU AND I
Similarities and differences | 69

OUR FAMILY
Sweet memories | 71

I *long to put the experience of fifty years at once into your young lives, to give you at once the key of that treasure chamber every gem of which has cost me tears and struggles and prayers, but you must work for these inward treasures yourselves.*

— HARRIET BEECHER STOWE

To My Daughter,

*T*his is a journal about you and me, mother and daughter. It's my gift to you. It may be the most precious gift I will ever be able to give you. I've filled it with love and the important recollections of a lifetime to help you understand who I am and why you've become the special person you are. It's my hope you will want to read this book from time to time whenever you'd like to reminisce. Each event I've written about, every feeling, is a piece in the intricate mosaic which is our relationship. I don't know why some memories shine like bright pennies and others dim and disappear, but they do. It's the bright shining pennies of our life together that I've written about.

With Love,

About My Mother

My mother's apron pockets were crammed with important objects. . . . an assortment of barrettes, marbles and puzzle pieces awaiting return to their 'proper places'; shoe laces which I had tied in triple knots and strung from the handle on my dresser's top drawer to the knob on my closet and back again. Why are tiny fragments like these among my favorite recollections of my mother? Why is it so important to include her in a book dedicated to my daughter? Because she is part of me and you. Our story cannot be complete without her.

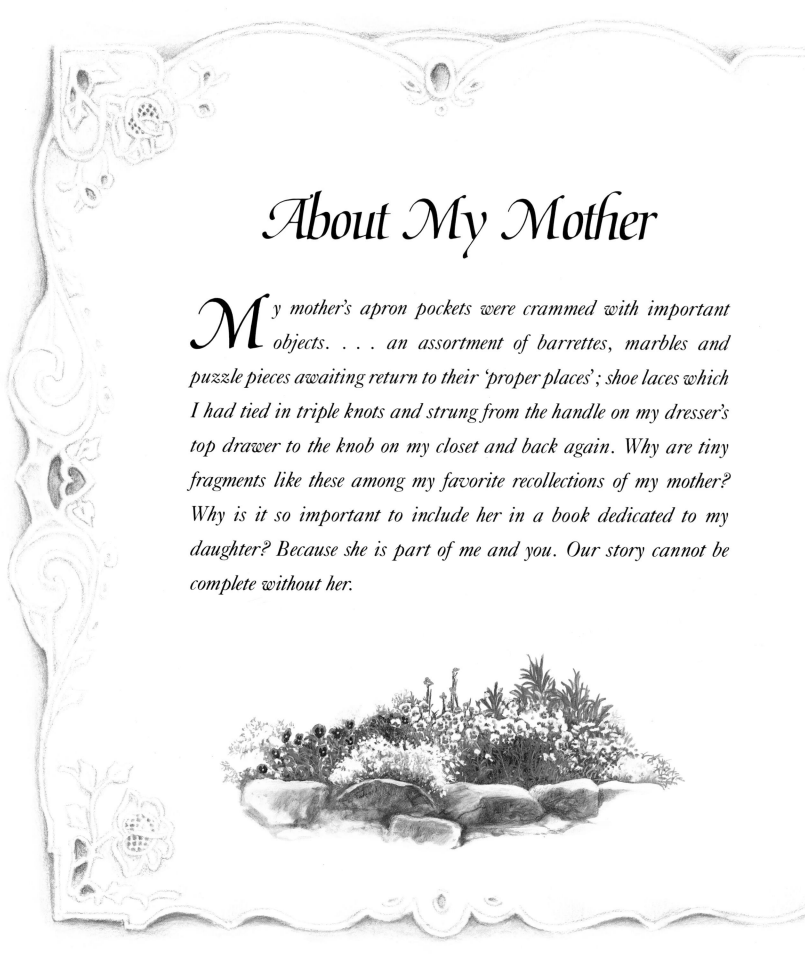

Her maiden name

_____

Who she was named after

_____

What her name means

_____

Her special grandmother name

_____

*Her
birth
date*

MY
FAVORITE
PHOTOGRAPH
OF HER

*Her
birthplace*

_____

_____

*N*obody knows of the work it makes
To keep the home together,
Nobody knows of the steps it takes,
Nobody knows—but mother.

— ANON

9

In the Beginning

*A*s a child I marveled at how my mother knew just how to mend my scraped knees, was always there with a handkerchief to end my sniffles, and had the uncanny ability to read my mind. She put on that knowing smile and I knew I was safe in her keeping. As long as she was nearby all would be right in the world. A good night kiss, her encouraging smile, her wisdom, the softness of her embrace, the scent of her as she'd come into a room . . . these are tucked lovingly among my childhood souvenirs. Mom always knew how many peas were left on my plate, and whether or not I had used toothpaste. She seemed to know when I was really sick or was just hoping to avoid another math test. And when I felt like the whole world was against me she was there to say "I know you can do it."

My earliest memories of my mother

_____

_____

_____

What she looked like when I was young

_____

_____

_____

What her personality was like

_____

_____

_____

What made her special to me

_____

_____

_____

Reflections

My mother didn't just spell out her philosophy, she left me to observe and draw my own conclusions. She probably knew I wasn't really listening, but watching. It didn't come to me all at once but eventually I was able to put into words what I believed to be the essential woman. I'd like *you* to understand what I admired about her.

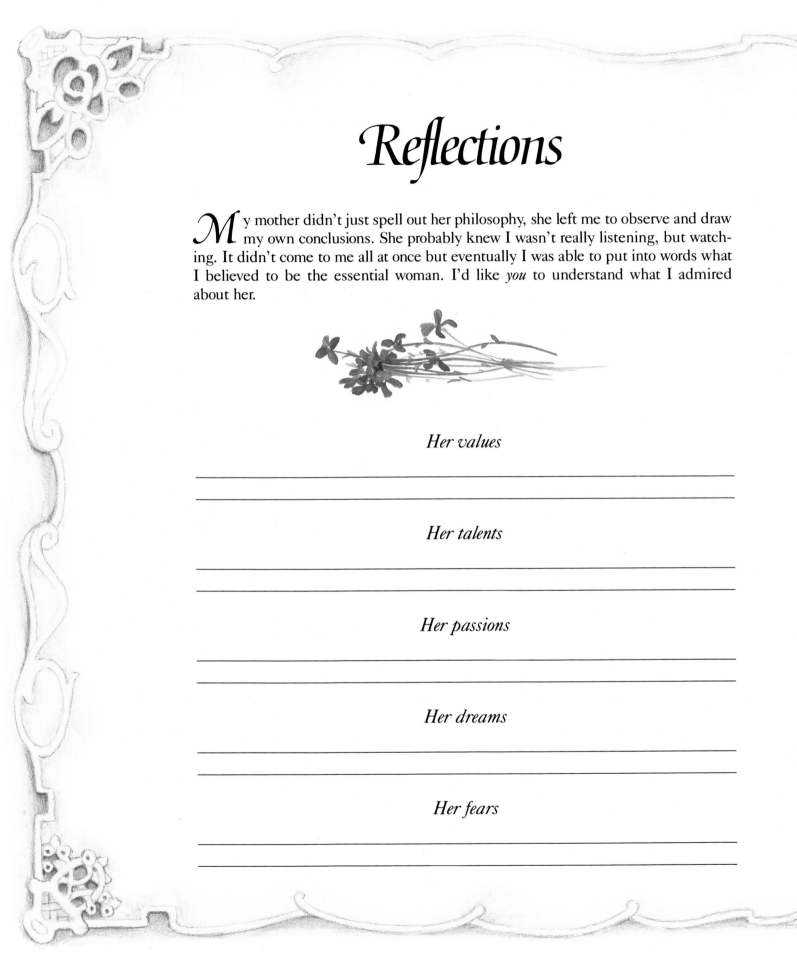

Her values

_____

_____

Her talents

_____

_____

Her passions

_____

_____

Her dreams

_____

_____

Her fears

_____

_____

I Remember

They say you can know a person by the friends she keeps. But surely favorite books, authors and many other things are equally our "friends." They too provide comfort and sometimes, even encouragement. These are some of the things that were among my mother's favorites. It's impossible for me to think of them without being reminded of her.

MY MOTHER'S FAVORITE

Color
_____

Scent
_____

Season
_____

Flower
_____

Place
_____

Person
_____

Book
_____

Writer
_____

Music
_____

Poem
_____
_____
_____
_____
_____
_____
_____

Becoming a Woman

I loved listening to my mother's tales about growing up. What stories she would tell! When she was a young girl, her family was the centerpiece of her life, her universe extending no more than a short distance from the house in which she grew up. *Her* mother's ambitions for her were limited to such domesticities as learning to cook, to sew, to garden, to 'keep house'—that's what proper young ladies did. But despite all of the built-in restraints of that time, there burned inside that girl—my mother—a desire to overcome her natural shyness and test herself beyond the frontier of family life. She did, and I'm so proud of her, and thankful for the courage she taught me.

My mother's best story about growing up

_____

_____

_____

Her closest girlhood friends

_____   _____

_____   _____

Her greatest 'victory'

_____

_____

_____

Her dreams for the future

_____

_____

_____

Autumn to winter, winter into spring,
Spring into summer, summer into fall,—
So rolls the changing year, and so we change;
Motion so swift, we know not that we move.

— DINAH MULOCK CRAIK

15

Once Upon a Time

"What was it like in the old days, Mommy?" How many times has a daughter put that question to a perplexed mother who then has to quickly realign her perspective from contemporary 'woman-of-the-world' to historical relic? "No, my love, we didn't have calculators, but I'm sure we did have electricity. No, I wasn't around when the automobile was invented but I do recall staying up all night to watch the first moon landing." Exactly when did the "olden days" leave off anyway? I suppose I was as guilty as every daughter of making my mother wince when I asked about wagon trains and cowboys. But, truth be told, life *was* incredibly different when my mother was a girl. Would you believe . . .

How women dressed

_____

_____

_____

How they were expected to behave

_____

_____

_____

What they did for entertainment

_____

_____

_____

What they were expected to become

_____

_____

_____

The past is a foreign country: they do things differently there.
— L.P. HARTLEY

Love & Marriage

Wvhen I grew older, my interests began to include romance. In my mind, my mother and father must have had a whirlwind courtship, a fairy-tale wedding, and an unforgettably romantic honeymoon. I would plead with my mother for details but could elicit them only in small doses. But every now and then we would sit down for a "talk," which meant she would fold her legs under her while her face took on a quiet glow as she remembered for me . . . and for herself.

How my parents met

_____

_____

What attracted my mother to my father

_____

_____

The Proposal

_____

_____

What my mother told me about her wedding day

_____

_____

_____

Date   *Place*

_____   _____

Her closest friends attending

_____   _____

_____   _____

W*hoso loves believes the impossible.*
— E L I Z A B E T H   B A R R E T T
B R O W N I N G

W*ith this ring, I thee wed,*
With my body I thee worship,
And with my worldly goods I thee endow.
— B O O K   O F   C O M M O N   P R A Y E R

Recollections

When I think about growing up with my mother, it's all the little things about her that pop into my mind. Most seem unimportant by themselves but there are so many, I realize how closely I must have been observing her. I knew instinctively how she would react to almost anything I said—whether she would smile or frown or say nothing. These are some of my best memories of those days.

Her finest quality

_____

_____

_____

Her happiest moment

_____

_____

_____

A day I'll never forget

_____

_____

_____

_____

The most surprising thing she ever did

_____

_____

_____

Our favorite time together

_____

_____

_____

Regrets

The bitterest tears shed over graves are for words left unsaid and deeds left undone.
—HARRIET BEECHER STOWE

What I never told my mother

_____

_____

What I would undo if I could

_____

_____

What I wish she had told me

_____

_____

My Mother's Kitchen

There we were, side by side, tasting, creating, giggling and having fun. Those were the days! "What do you think it needs?" she would ask. "More chocolate," I invariably replied, even if we were making a roast. Or she would plead, "I can't figure out how much is three quarters of a cup." That's how I learned fractions. My mother's kitchen was a place for solving problems. Whenever I had something especially difficult to discuss I would wait until we were baking bread. Then, she would just listen, not saying much. But I could tell how she felt by watching the way she kneaded—should I say pounded—the dough.

My most vivid recollection of my mother's kitchen

_____

_____

_____

_____

My mother's very best recipe

_____   _____

_____   _____

_____   _____

_____   _____

_____   _____

_____   _____

There was nothing remote or mysterious here—only something private. The only secret was the ancient communication between two people.

— EUDORA WELTY

And the best bread was of my mother's own making—the best in all the land! — HENRY JAMES

No mean woman can cook well for it calls for a light head, a generous spirit and a large heart. — PAUL GAUGUIN

My Mother's Wisdom

My mother didn't consider herself wise, but whether she knew it or not, she *was* a teacher. Her greatest course was Courage 101. The lessons were always delivered quietly and without embellishment, "Follow your heart, nothing's impossible." Or, she would encourage, "Don't hold back; the real tragedy isn't failure, but wondering what might have been."

Words that still ring in my ears

_____

_____

_____

What I learned from her example

_____

_____

_____

Advice given but not taken

_____

_____

_____

Mama *exhorted her children at every opportunity to "jump at de sun." We might not land on the sun, but at least we would get off the ground.*
— ZORA NEALE HURSTON

It seems to me we can never give up longing and wishing while we are thoroughly alive. There are certain things we feel to be beautiful and good, and we <u>must</u> hunger after them.

— GEORGE ELIOT

Risk! Risk anything! Care no more for the opinion of others, for those voices. Do the hardest thing on earth for you. Act for yourself. Face the truth.

— KATHERINE MANSFIELD

You must do the thing you think you cannot do.

— ELEANOR ROOSEVELT

Courage is the price that life exacts for granting peace.
The soul that knows it not, knows no release
From little things;
Knows not the livid loneliness of fear.

— AMELIA EARHART

If we had no winter, the spring would not be so pleasant: if we did not sometimes taste of adversity, prosperity would not be so welcome.

— ANNE BRADSTREET

Never grow a wishbone, daughter, where your backbone ought to be.

— CLEMENTINE PADDLEFORD

Places of the Heart

*I*can still see her there occupying her favorite spot, bursting with quiet industry, reflecting on things I knew little about. I understand now that everyone needs somewhere to go where dreams find wings, where lessons are absorbed, where tomorrows are considered, and where inner peace is possible. Now, whenever I think of my mother, I cannot separate her from that special place.

How I would describe her special place

_____

_____

_____

What we did there together

_____

_____

_____

How she spent her private moments there

_____

_____

_____

_____

MY MOTHER'S GARDEN

LEAVES FROM
The Language of Flowers

ANGELICA	CLEMATIS	JASMINE
Inspiration	*Beautiful thoughts*	*Amiability*
CAMOMILE	HOLLY	SWEET VIOLET
Energy in adversity	*Foresight*	*Modesty*
CEDAR	HONEY SUCKLE	WATER LILY
Strength	*Sweet disposition*	*Purity of heart*

My Mother's Gifts

Maybe it's in the way you tilt your head when perplexed, or that slow sweet smile of yours. Perhaps it's in the determination you show whenever faced with a difficult situation. Whatever it is, sometimes you remind me so much of your grandmother.

What I most want you to understand about my mother

_____

_____

_____

The things you do that remind me of her

_____

_____

_____

The talents you and I inherited from her

_____

_____

_____

She was the last of the generation of real grandmothers. One of the women who made a special grace of age. —HELEN HAYES
[about her maternal grandmother]

Grandma was a kind of first-aid station, or a Red Cross nurse, who took up where the battle ended, accepting us and our little sobbing sins, gathering the whole of us into her lap, restoring us to health and confidence by her amazing faith in life and in a mortal's strength to meet it. —LILLIAN SMITH

About Myself

I remember reaching an age when images of my future began to take shape in my mind. It happened almost overnight. I had been content wearing jeans, climbing trees and never giving a thought to the next day. Suddenly I wanted only pretty clothes and a clear-cut blueprint into the future. One day I would imagine becoming a ballerina, the next day I wanted to raise horses. Sometimes I visualized myself traveling the world, other times spending my days in a small cottage with a thatched roof and a cozy fireplace. Would I be an actress or a teacher? Would I fall in love? I felt I must decide, like choosing a hat off the shelf, and I ignored my mother's advice to "remain true to yourself and the rest will follow." Are you surprised to hear I was once the most confused person anyone ever met? Well, there's more that might surprise you, so read on.

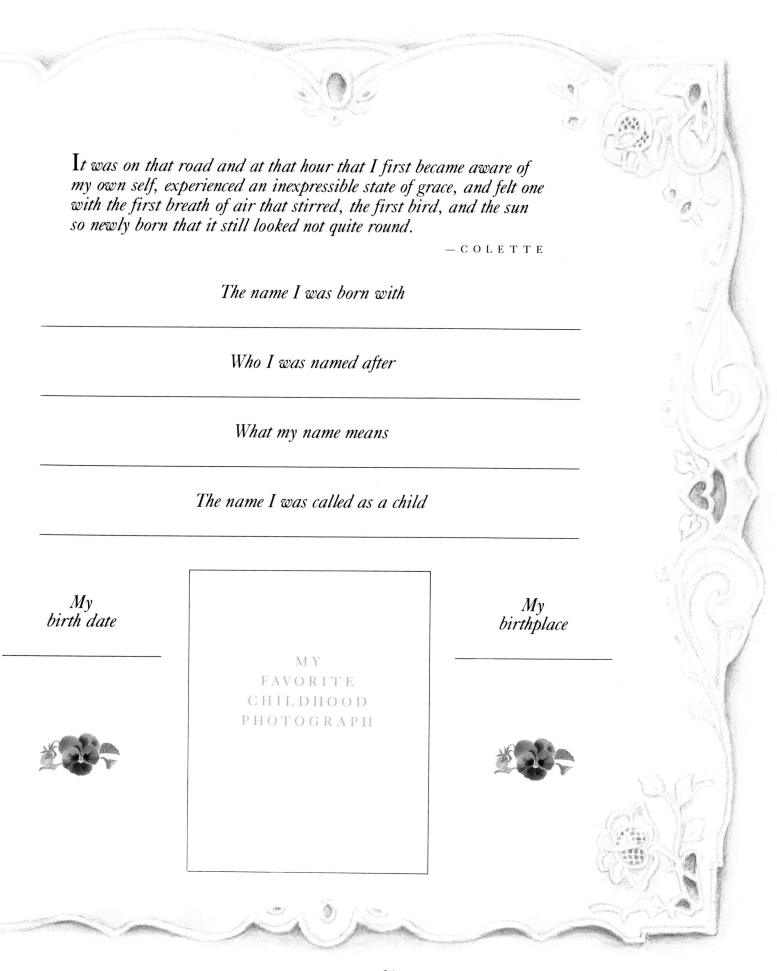

It was on that road and at that hour that I first became aware of my own self, experienced an inexpressible state of grace, and felt one with the first breath of air that stirred, the first bird, and the sun so newly born that it still looked not quite round.

— COLETTE

The name I was born with

_____

Who I was named after

_____

What my name means

_____

The name I was called as a child

_____

*My
birth date*

*My
birthplace*

MY
FAVORITE
CHILDHOOD
PHOTOGRAPH

The popular idea that a child forgets easily is not an accurate one.
Many people go right through life in the grip of an idea which has
been impressed on them in very tender years.

— AGATHA CHRISTIE

When I Was Very Young

Everything seemed big. Grownups towered over me so that I had to stretch my neck to look up. I remember wondering what was on top of the refrigerator, thinking, "Someday, I'll be tall enough to find out what's up there." But I knew I was little, so I could never understand why my mother's friends would always greet me with "My goodness, how big you are."

My earliest recollections

_____

_____

_____

The story about me told most often

_____

_____

_____

My most embarrassing moment as a young child

_____

_____

_____

Warmest memories of those years

_____

_____

_____

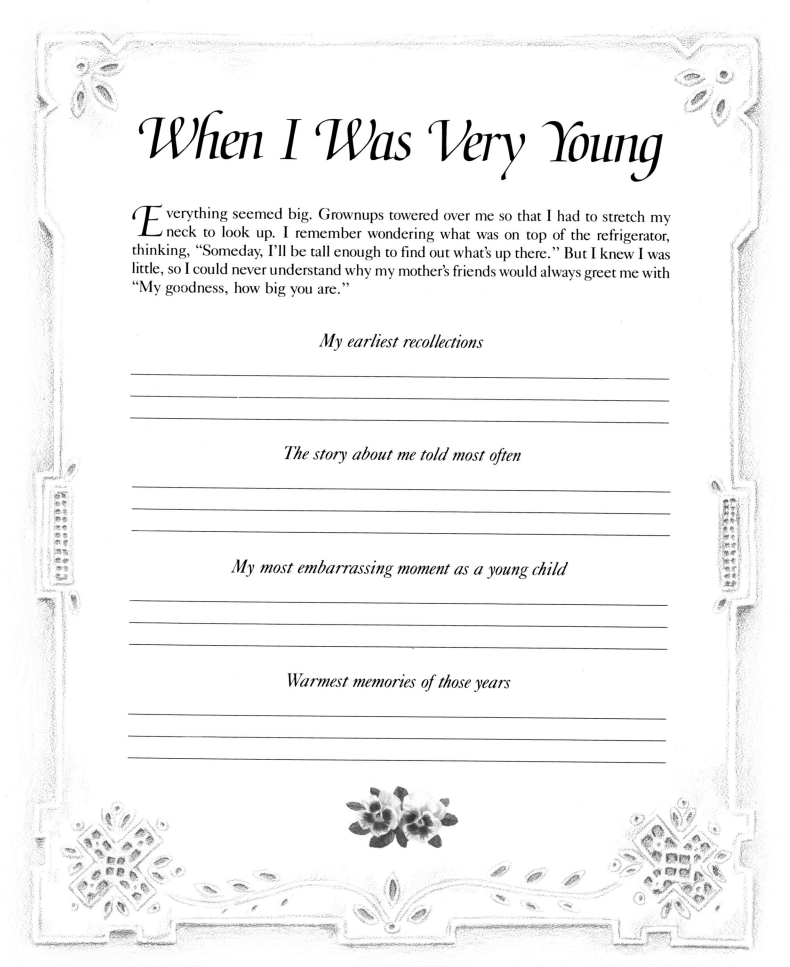

Mid pleasures and palaces though we may roam,
Be it ever so humble, there's no place like home.

—JOHN HOWARD PAYNE

34

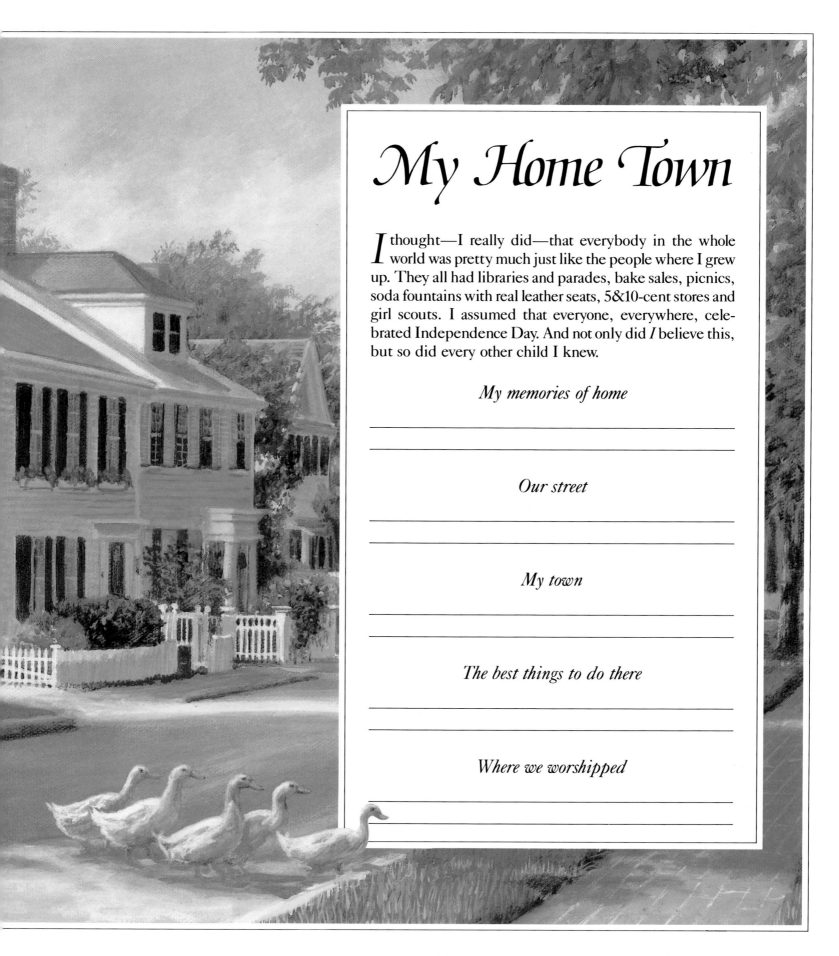

My Home Town

I thought—I really did—that everybody in the whole world was pretty much just like the people where I grew up. They all had libraries and parades, bake sales, picnics, soda fountains with real leather seats, 5&10-cent stores and girl scouts. I assumed that everyone, everywhere, celebrated Independence Day. And not only did *I* believe this, but so did every other child I knew.

My memories of home

_____

_____

Our street

_____

_____

My town

_____

_____

The best things to do there

_____

_____

Where we worshipped

_____

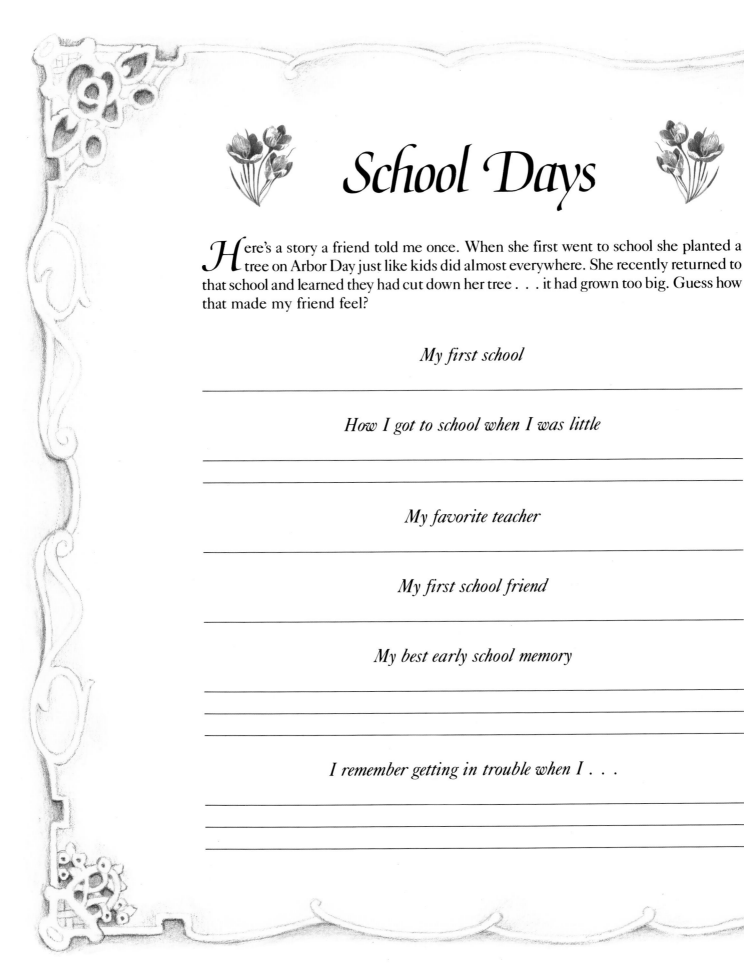

School Days

*H*ere's a story a friend told me once. When she first went to school she planted a tree on Arbor Day just like kids did almost everywhere. She recently returned to that school and learned they had cut down her tree . . . it had grown too big. Guess how that made my friend feel?

My first school

_____

How I got to school when I was little

_____
_____

My favorite teacher

_____

My first school friend

_____

My best early school memory

_____
_____
_____

I remember getting in trouble when I . . .

_____
_____
_____

 # After School

*E*very day after school I would be met by my faithful friend Gypsy, the black cocker spaniel who never seemed to mind when I dressed her in sun bonnets and frilly dresses and crawled into her basket. When I went to kindergarten Gypsy would see me to the door in the morning and greet me at the door on my return. Those were the days.

My first best friend

_____

_____

_____

My favorite toy or doll I would give anything for if only it could be found

_____

_____

_____

My favorite "read aloud" bedtime story

_____

_____

_____

My warmest childhood memory

_____

_____

_____

Civilization is cruel in sending [children] off to bed at the stimulating time of dusk. —ALICE MEYNELL

To make a prairie it takes
a clover and one bee,
One clover, and a bee,
And revery.
The revery alone will do,
If bees are few.
— EMILY DICKINSON

Daydreams

When I was still quite young, according to my mother, patience was not my virtue. It belonged to other mothers' little girls. I was the girl who was always in a hurry to play baseball with the boys. Or I rushed through my homework so there would be time for climbing trees and having chestnut wars or eating all the cherries and getting sick. Then one day, like a flash, I slowed down. I began to spend hours just thinking and dreaming about what might be. Does any of this sound familiar? It should.

I could spend hours just thinking about

_____

_____

The best scheme I ever hatched

_____

_____

My dreams about growing up

_____

_____

All things are possible until they are proved impossible—and even the impossible may only be so, as of now.

—PEARL S. BUCK

One can never consent to creep when one feels an impulse to soar.

—HELEN KELLER

My Room

*M*y room was my safe haven. There I could play *my* music, hang *my* pictures, collect *my* stuff—and rearrange *my* closet into umpteen new outfits. There I could stare out of my window onto my future while looking out over the houses nearby and feeling safe and secure. I don't think I have ever since felt so protected.

What my room looked like

_____
_____
_____

The view from my window

_____
_____

I loved collecting

_____
_____
_____

My truly private thoughts

_____
_____
_____

*D*ear Mother: I'm all right. Stop worrying about me.
—EGYPTIAN PAPYRUS LETTER
C. 2000 BC

Dear Diary

My diaries were written primarily, I think, not to preserve the experience but to savor it, to make it even more real, more visible and palpable, than in actual life. For in our family an experience was not finished, not truly experienced, unless written down or shared with another. — ANNE MORROW LINDBERGH

My deepest darkest secret

_____

_____

What I knew that would have surprised my parents

_____

_____

How I viewed grownups

_____

_____

How (I thought) grownups looked at me

_____

_____

Because after a time having a secret and nobody knowing you have a secret is no fun. And although you don't want others to know what the secret is, you want them to at least know you have one. — E.L. KONIGSBURG

Boys

Did you ever stop to consider how when you're five years old you get along just fine with boys. But soon they start pulling your hair and playing war so you play with dolls. Then they start to like you again but not your dolls. Its a difficult choice.

The first boy I ever noticed who noticed me back.

_____

_____

My first date

_____

_____

_____

My first boyfriend

_____

_____

My best boyfriend

_____

_____

What I learned that I'd like you to know

_____

_____

_____

"Boyfriends" weren't friends at all; they were prizes, escorts, symbols of achievement, fascinating strangers, the Other.
— SUSAN ALLEN TOTH

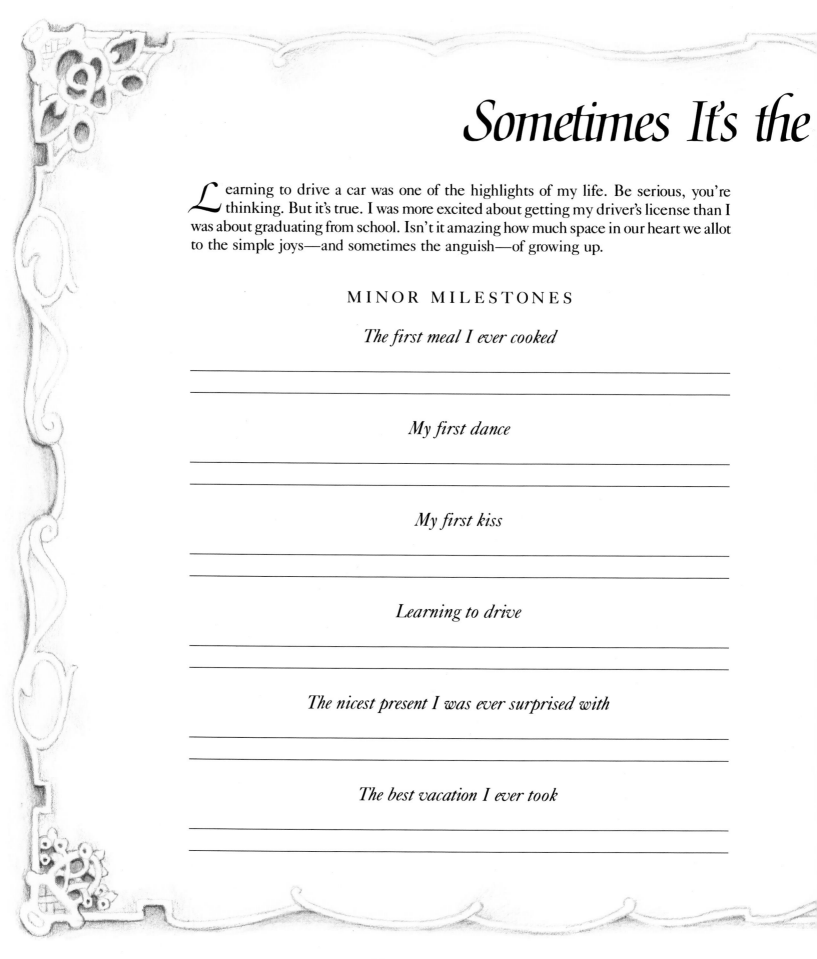

Sometimes It's the

Learning to drive a car was one of the highlights of my life. Be serious, you're thinking. But it's true. I was more excited about getting my driver's license than I was about graduating from school. Isn't it amazing how much space in our heart we allot to the simple joys—and sometimes the anguish—of growing up.

MINOR MILESTONES

The first meal I ever cooked

_____

_____

My first dance

_____

_____

My first kiss

_____

_____

Learning to drive

_____

_____

The nicest present I was ever surprised with

_____

_____

The best vacation I ever took

_____

_____

Little Things

My most important birthday

_____

_____

Graduation, at last

_____

_____

My first job

_____

_____

My first car

_____

_____

My one shining moment

_____

_____

The most meaningful award I ever received

_____

_____

My worst story

_____

_____

My Passions

*"And what are you reading . . . ?" "Oh! it is only a novel" . . .
or, in short, only some work in which the most thorough knowledge
of human nature, the happiest delineation of its varieties, the
liveliest effusions of wit and humour are conveyed to the world in
the best chosen language.*
—JANE AUSTEN

MY FAVORITE

Book

_____

Writer

_____

Color

_____

Scent

_____

Season

_____

Flower

_____

Pastime

_____

Music

_____

Wonderful Words

Sometimes someone writes a book, a poem, a passage, and the words strike such a chord inside that they become like friends. There's security in knowing that they're always there, able to provide warmth and encouragement whenever needed. It's as if some complete stranger, some writer who may even be dead, who knows nothing about you, understands you completely. Over the course of my life, these are the written words that have meant the most to me.

_____
_____
_____
_____
_____
_____
_____
_____
_____
_____
_____
_____
_____
_____
_____
_____
_____
_____
_____
_____

EMILY
DICKINSON

*A word is dead
When it is said,
Some say.
I say it just
Begins to live
That day.*

If I read a book and it makes my whole body so cold no fire can ever warm me, I know __that__ is poetry. If I feel physically as if the top of my head were taken off, I know __that__ is poetry. These are the only ways I know it. Is there any other way?

Love Conquers All

. . . I have for the first time found what I can truly love—I have found you. You are my sympathy—my better self—my good angel—I am bound to you with a strong attachment. I think you good, gifted, lovely: a fervent, a solemn passion is conceived in my heart; it leans to you, draws you to my centre and spring of life, wraps my existence about you—and kindling in pure, powerful flame, fuses you and me in one.
—CHARLOTTE BRONTË

How I met your father

_____
_____

What attracted me to him

_____
_____
_____
_____

Recollections of our courtship

_____
_____
_____

The Proposal

_____
_____
_____

My Wedding

The bridegroom's hand trembled visibly and no one heard his replies, but Meg looked straight up into her husband's eyes and said, "I will!" with such tender trust in her own face and voice that Aunt March sniffed audibly. —LOUISA MAY ALCOTT

The date I was married

_____

Where we were married

_____

What I wore

_____

_____

My Maid of Honor

_____

The Best Man

_____

Memories of my wedding day

_____

_____

_____

Where we went on our honeymoon

_____

49

I *begin to love this little creature, and to anticipate [her] birth as a fresh twist to a knot, which I do not wish to untie.*

— MARY WOLLSTONECRAFT

Then There Was You

I'll never forget when I learned you were living inside me. I looked in the mirror and somehow I just knew. There is no way to describe the completeness a woman feels when she knows another heart beats under her own. I felt so blessed, so important. With your first little kick I visualized us dancing around the room. There would be nothing I wouldn't do for you . . . my little miracle!

My mother's reaction

_____

_____

Your father's first words

_____

_____

My memories of the day you were born

_____

_____

The feelings I experienced that moment I first held you

_____

_____

Who you resembled

_____

_____

About My Daughter

That day, the day you were born, was the most exhilarating day of my life. Ask me how I spent the morning, ask who came to call, ask me anything about that day and I'll know. Every detail. Most of all I remember how beautiful you looked. I was so proud of you and me. I should have been filled with doubts about whether I could do right by you but, on the contrary, I knew I was ready! I had a plan. I would love you too much; I would protect you for a while; I would teach you how to fly on your own. You might leave my nest, my daughter, but if I did my job well you'd be back, as my friend.

The name you were born with

_____

Who you were named after

_____

What your name means

_____

Your birth date *Time of birth* *Your birth place*

_____

What you looked like

_____
_____

MY
FAVORITE
CHILDHOOD
PHOTOGRAPH
OF YOU

. . .*Who is getting more pleasure from this rocking, the baby or me?*
— NANCY THAYER

When You Were A Little Girl

*T*iny little tears rolled down your cheeks as you ran into my arms like a mouse escaping the night owl. I wrapped you in protection, yet each time telling myself "teach her to clad herself in armor and be brave. I must remember to love her enough to let her fall."

Your little idiosyncrasies that made me smile

_____

_____

Your humorous expressions

_____

_____

Your first gift to me

_____

_____

Your first party

_____

_____

Adventures at bedtime

_____

_____

What feeling is so nice as a child's hand in yours? So small, so soft and warm, like a kitten huddling in the shelter of your clasp.

— MARJORIE HOLMES

First Wings

O n your first day of school, you stood there on the bottom step all dressed up in the clothes you had tried on at least ten times over the past few days. With shiny new shoes and not a hair out of place, where was the precious little baby I had rocked to sleep only yesterday? You turned, gave me a big grin, and said, "Bye Mom, I love you." I stood there waving and smiling, crying like a fool. You were so anxious to grow up. Can you remember . . .

The name of your first school

_____

What that first day was like

_____

_____

Your favorite teacher

_____

Where we lived

_____

How you got to school

_____

_____

Your first best friend

_____

It will be gone before you know it. The fingerprints on the wall appear higher and higher. Then suddenly they disappear.

— D O R O T H Y   E V S L I N

Later On

"Mom, can I have a friend over?" were the first words you uttered each day upon returning from a hard day of counting from one to a hundred in Mrs. Sweeney's class. Not to be outsmarted by a five year old, I invariably replied "Have you picked up your room?" This ritual served as our daily afternoon greeting for quite a while and might have left me with feelings of inadequacy if I hadn't learned that *I* should also count to one hundred. By the time I finished you would walk back into my room, smile, throw your arms around me and say, "I love you, Mommy."

Your favorite toy

_____

The game you always beat me at

_____

That special doll

_____

Our most wonderful pet

_____

Bedtime stories you loved

_____
_____
_____

Special Memories, Special Years

Teenagers are people who express a burning desire to be different by dressing exactly alike.
                                                                    — A N O N

Your friends I loved

_____

_____

Your opinion of boys

_____

_____

Their opinion of you

_____

_____

What came easily for you then

_____

_____

What was difficult

_____

_____

My proudest moment

_____

_____

Mom's Apple Pie

Do you remember the hours we spent in the kitchen together? The aromas, licking the spoon when we were done, grandma's secret recipes, the closeness. Who can forget the mess, all those broken egg shells; the time I used salt instead of sugar; the cookie dough you made into clay by kneading it with too much flour. Well, my dearest, here are those recipes we loved making together. *Guard them with your life!*

_____

Cooking is like love. It should be entered into with abandon or not at all.

— HARRIET VAN HORNE

All Grown Up

*T*hen one day you floated down the stairs in crinoline and lace, a butterfly at last. What happened to gangly legs, to picture books and climbing trees? It seemed too soon, but your shy smile and contented look made me remember what it was like to become a woman. Recollections of those years flood my memories. I especially like to recall . . .

_____

_____

_____

_____

_____

_____

_____

_____

_____

_____

_____

_____

_____

_____

These are my daughters, I suppose.
But where in the world did the children vanish?

— PHYLLIS MCGINLEY

When We Became Friends

I suppose it was the day I sought your advice, that time I brought my problem to you instead of the other way around. You didn't seem surprised. You just asked questions, woman to woman, to help you understand my predicament better. You behaved like a friend who was truly interested. Then you offered suggestions, good ones. I could feel your empathy. I didn't even realize what had occurred—that we had passed a milestone—until later, did you?

What's most important to me about our friendship

_____

_____

_____

_____

_____

_____

_____

_____

Shared joy is double joy, and shared sorrow is half sorrow.
— SWEDISH PROVERB

. . . The daughter is for the mother at once her double and another person.
— SIMONE DE BEAUVOIR

We are together, my child and I. Mother and child, yes, but sisters really, against whatever denies us all that we are.

— ALICE WALKER

Mr. Right

Oh, / I am thinking / Oh, / I am thinking
I have found / my lover / Oh, / I think it is so.
—CHIPPEWA SONG

What I felt when I first met the man of your dreams

_____

_____

What your father and I discussed later

_____

_____

What you were like after he proposed

_____

_____

PHOTO

Your Wedding

If ever two were one, than surely we.
If ever man were loved by wife, then thee.
—ANNE BRADSTREET

Your wedding date

_____

Where you were married

_____

Your husband's full name

_____

Your wedding dress

_____
_____

What I wore

_____
_____

My feelings on that day of days

_____
_____
_____
_____
_____

Whatever our souls are made of, his and mine are the same.
—EMILY BRONTË

The Best of Times

There's a game I sometimes play. I pretend that I can replay the really special days of our lives. Do you remember that incredibly beautiful day at the beach, the time when we spent hours building sand castles? You were so young, yet it seems like only yesterday. Or, the day you were married. Was there ever a more radiant bride? Let me play back for you now some of my fondest recollections. Do you remember . . .

_____

_____

_____

_____

_____

_____

_____

_____

_____

Make a memory with your children,
Spend some time to show you care;
Toys and trinkets can't replace those
Precious moments that you share.
— ELAINE HARDT

. . . The companions of our childhood always possess a certain
power over our minds which hardly any later friend can obtain.

— MARY SHELLEY

Private Thoughts

*H*ere is my recipe for a happy life; the ingredients are simple. First, know yourself; you'll always know what to do next when difficulties arise. Second, live in the present; savor every minute because time is what we have least of. Third, never stop learning. One of the surprises of growing older is that the mind doesn't. Fourth, stay as wonderful as you are.

My dreams for you

_____

_____

_____

How you changed my life

_____

_____

_____

What you've taught me

_____

_____

_____

What I've learned from life

_____

_____

_____

*T*here were many ways of breaking a heart. Stories were full of hearts being broken by love, but what really broke a heart was taking away its dream—whatever that dream might be.

— PEARL S. BUCK

68

You & I

There's a special relationship between mothers and daughters. They can be like identical twins yet completely different. When I was a girl I watched my mother and adopted the bits and pieces of her that fit. You've done the same with me. I see it in so many ways. But don't think I'm hoping for a carbon copy. You have your own wonderful talents. It's your time now . . . seize the day.

How you're like me

_____

_____

_____

How we're different

_____

_____

_____

How you are completely different from anyone I've ever met

_____

_____

_____

Being with you is like walking on a very clear morning—definitely the sensation of belonging there.

— A N O N

Mary and Laura pulled out two small packages. They unwrapped them, and each found a little heart-shaped cake. Over their delicate brown tops was sprinkled white sugar. The sparkling grains lay like tiny drifts of snow.
　　　　　　　　　　　　　　　　　　　—LAURA INGALLS WILDER

Our Family

*W*e all gather once again—young and old, introvert and life-of-the-party, freckled cousins and smiling grandmothers whose eyes brim with pride and happy memories. What would the day be without brothers, dads and sons sharing the latest jokes and achievements. It is a time for the family to reaffirm itself and grow, to bond with newlyweds and precious little ones, to reminisce about loved ones lost. It's a day to laugh and hug and remember who we are.

Memories of our family life

_____

_____

_____

_____

Our most important traditions

_____

_____

_____

_____

How we celebrated the holidays

_____

_____

_____

_____

The family—that dear octopus from whose tentacles we never quite escape, nor, in our inmost hearts, ever quite wish to.
— DODIE SMITH

Acknowledgements

Every effort has been made to locate the copyright holders of materials used in this book. Should there be any omissions or errors, we apologize and shall be pleased to make the appropriate acknowledgements in future editions.

Grateful acknowledgement is made to the following for permission to reprint previously published material: Little, Brown and Company, for permission to reprint "To make a prairie it takes a clover and one bee" and "A word is dead" from *THE COMPLETE WORKS OF EMILY DICKINSON*, edited by Thomas H. Johnson; Little, Brown and Company for permission to excerpt from *BLOOMING: A SMALL-TOWN GIRLHOOD* by Susan Allen Toth; HarperCollins Publishers Inc. for permission to quote from *DUST TRACKS ON A ROAD* by Zora Neale Hurston, copyright © 1942 by Zora Neale Hurston, copyright renewed 1970 by John C. Hurston; Farrar, Straus & Giroux, Inc. for permission to excerpt from *MY MOTHER'S HOUSE AND SIDO* by Colette, copyright © 1953 by Farrar, Straus & Young, copyright renewed © 1981 by Farrar, Straus & Giroux, Inc; Alfred A. Knopf, Inc. for permission to excerpt two passages from *THE SECOND SEX* by Simone de Beauvoir, copyright © 1952 by Alfred A. Knopf, Inc. and renewed © 1980 by Alfred A. Knopf, Inc.; Harold Ober Associates Inc. for permission to excerpt from *A BRIDGE FOR PASSING* by Pearl S. Buck, copyright © 1962 by Pearl S. Buck, copyright renewed 1990 by Pearl S. Buck, and from *THE PATRIOT* by Pearl S. Buck, copyright © 1939 by Pearl S. Buck, copyright renewed 1966 by Pearl S. Buck; Doubleday, a division of Bantam Doubleday Dell Publishing Group, Inc., for permission to excerpt from *THE OPEN DOOR* by Helen Keller, copyright © 1957 by Helen Keller.